Contents

MANCHESTER LIBRARIES (UK) WITHDRAWN FROM STOCK

D1323248

Animals and people in the story

Buck   Spitz   Dave

Perrault and François   John Thornton

Hal, Charles, and Mercedes

New words

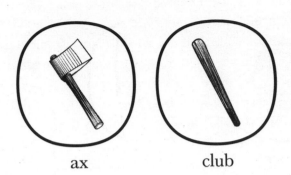

ax   club

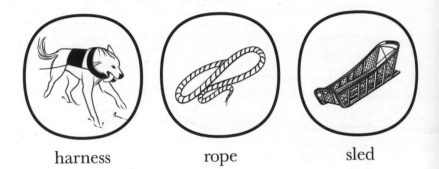

harness   rope   sled

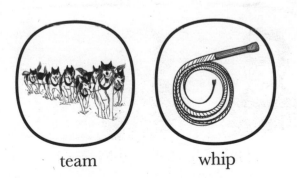

team   whip

Note about the story

Jack London was a famous American writer. He loved **life*** in the **wild** and wrote many stories about the people and animals there. In 1897, people found **gold** in the Klondike in north-west Canada. Thousands of people went there, and London went there, too. The people needed a lot of big, strong dogs for the difficult **journey**. *The Call of the Wild* (1903) is the story of one of those dogs—Buck.

Before-reading questions

1 Look at the cover of the book, then look quickly at the pictures in the book. Are these sentences about the story *true* or *false*?

   a The story happens in Africa.

   b The story is about a ship.

   c The story happens in a cold country.

   d There are no animals in the story.

   e There are animals and people in the story.

2 Look at the man and dog in the picture on page 10 of the story. What is happening?

3 Some people say a dog is "a man's best friend." Why do people say this, do you think?

4 Some dogs work. What work do they do?

*Definitions of words in **bold** can be found in the glossary on pages 62–63.

CHAPTER ONE
The man with the club

Buck was a big, strong dog with **thick**, warm fur. He was four years old, and he lived with a rich family in a big house in California.

Buck was part of the family, and everybody loved him. He played with the children and carried them on his back. In summer, he swam with them in the river. On cold winter nights, he lay in front of the fire and slept. His **life** was happy and easy.

But, one day, everything changed for Buck. In 1897, people heard about **gold** in the Klondike, in north-west Canada. Men came from many countries. They hoped to find gold and **become** rich. These men needed dogs to work for them. It was very cold in the Klondike, and the men wanted big, strong dogs with thick fur.

A man called Manuel worked for Buck's family. Manuel needed money. Every day he watched the children playing with Buck. "People will pay a lot of money for Buck," he thought.

One night, Buck's family were away from home. Manuel took Buck to a strange part of town and met a man with a **rope**. The man **tied** the rope **around** Buck and gave Manuel some money. Then, the man pushed Buck into a big, strong box.

The next morning, four men carried the box on to a train. Buck stayed on the train for two days and two nights. Nobody brought him food or water. He was hungry, thirsty, and very angry!

The train stopped at the town of Seattle, and a man in a red shirt came to meet it. This man carried an **ax** and a **club**. Some men carried the box with Buck from the train. They put it down on the ground and sat on a high wall to watch.

The man in the red shirt came up to the box and started to hit it with the ax. Buck was now very, very angry. The box opened, and Buck ran out. He really wanted to **attack** the man. The man hit Buck with the club, hard. Buck **fell** to the ground. He got up, but the man hit him again. Blood ran from Buck's nose, mouth, and ears.

The man hit Buck again and again. After that, Buck could not **fight** any more. He lay on the ground and watched the man.

"Good dog, Buck," said the man. "You know your place now." He brought meat and water, and Buck ate and drank.

That day, Buck learned an important lesson. He could not fight a man with a club.

In the next days, many other dogs came. Some came in boxes, and others had ropes around them. All of them were very angry. Then, the man in the red shirt hit them with his club, and they became quiet.

Into the north

Sometimes, men came and talked to the man in the red shirt. They paid him money and took away some dogs. One day, a man called Perrault came to see the man in the red shirt. Perrault had an important job; he carried letters for the Canadian **Government**. He knew a lot about dogs, and when he saw Buck he was very happy.

"That's a very good dog!" Perrault said. "How much do you want for him?"

"Three hundred dollars," said the man in the red shirt.

Perrault paid the man and took Buck away to a ship. He also bought a dog called Curly. Another man, François, waited on the ship. He worked with Perrault. There were two other dogs on the ship—Spitz and Dave. Spitz was a big, white dog from Norway. At dinner, he tried to take Buck's food. But François hit him with a **whip**. Dave was a quiet dog, but he was not friendly. He liked to eat and sleep a lot.

The ship traveled north from Seattle. Every day, the weather grew colder. Then, one day, strange white things fell from the sky. Buck tried to eat them, but everybody laughed at him.

"You can't eat snow, Buck!" said François.

The ship stopped at Skagway in Alaska. It was very cold, and the snow was thick on the ground. There was a big **camp** there, with lots of men and dogs. Many of these dogs were big and **dangerous**.

Curly was a friendly dog. She ran toward one of the dogs to say hello. But the dog made an angry noise and attacked her. Curly fell on the ground, and Spitz, the big white dog, laughed at her. The other dogs ran toward Curly and attacked her. François came with an ax and the dogs ran away. But Curly was **dead**, and Spitz laughed again. After that, Buck **hated** Spitz.

The next day, François put a **harness** on Buck. Then, he tied all the dogs together in a **line**. François stood on a **sled**, and the dogs pulled him.

"That Buck is a very good dog," François said to Perrault. "He is strong, and he learns quickly."

Perrault bought more dogs. Their names were Joe, Billee, and Sol-leks. Joe and Billee were brothers, and Sol-leks was an old dog with only one eye. Then Perrault bought three more dogs; now he had a **team** of nine.

Perrault had to take important letters to Dawson City, hundreds of **miles** north, on the Yukon River. He put the letters into heavy bags on the sled, and the team left early the next morning. It was very cold, and the **journey** to Dawson was long and difficult. Every day, they traveled many miles through the snow. Perrault walked in front of the team, and François drove the dogs from the back.

Buck watched the other dogs and learned many new things from them. At night, the dogs slept under the snow. When they were thirsty, they **broke** the hard **ice** and drank the water under it.

In his home in the south, Buck never took food from people or other animals. But now he was always hungry because he worked hard. The men gave him fish, but he wanted more.

One day, Buck watched Pike, one of the new dogs. Pike took some meat from François, but François did not see him. The next day, Buck did the same thing. After that, he often took food from people and other dogs.

Spitz was the number-one dog in the line. Spitz hated Buck, and he always tried to attack him. Buck hated Spitz, too, but he did not want to fight him.

"One day, there's going to be a big **fight** between Spitz and Buck," said Perrault. "And Spitz will kill Buck."

"No," said François. "Buck will get angry and kill Spitz. I know it."

CHAPTER THREE
The big fight

Perrault knew a lot about ice. He knew when ice was "good" and when it was "bad". "Good" ice was thick and hard. The dogs could pull the heavy sled across it. But "bad" ice was very dangerous. It was **thin** and broke easily. One day, some bad ice broke, and Dave and Buck fell into the cold water. Perrault and François pulled them out quickly. Another day, Spitz fell through the ice and pulled some other dogs after him.

One cold, gray afternoon, after days of hard work, the team came to Dawson. Perrault, François, and the dogs rested for a week. But then they had to take more letters back to Skagway. Buck worked hard, and he enjoyed the work. But Spitz was the number-one dog, and he hated Buck. When he saw Buck, he made angry noises. He wanted to attack him and kill him.

One night, after dinner, one of the dogs saw a rabbit near the camp. The rabbit ran away, and all the dogs ran after it. Buck was nearest to the rabbit, with the other dogs behind him. Spitz left the other dogs, ran through some trees, and **jumped** out in front of the rabbit. Spitz caught the rabbit with his teeth and killed it easily.

Buck was very, very angry with Spitz. That was his rabbit! He jumped up at Spitz and attacked him. But Spitz was bigger and stronger. His teeth cut into Buck. Blood ran down Buck's head and body. The other dogs watched and waited. Buck attacked Spitz again and again. Then he broke Spitz's leg with his teeth. Now Spitz had only three legs. Then Buck attacked again and broke another leg. Spitz could not stand up, and he fell to the ground. All the other dogs ran toward him and killed him.

The next morning, Spitz was not in the camp. François looked at Buck. There were big cuts on his body, and François showed them to Perrault.

"Look," he said. "Spitz and Buck had a fight. Now Spitz is dead."

Perrault put Sol-leks in Spitz's place at the front of the line. But Buck wanted to be the number-one dog. He ran toward Sol-leks and pushed him away. Then he stood in Sol-leks's place.

"Look at Buck," said François. "He killed Spitz, and now he wants his job. Go back to your old place, Buck!" He pushed Buck away and put Sol-leks at the front again.

But Buck did not move, and François went to get a club. Buck remembered the man in the red shirt; he could not fight a man with a club. He ran through the camp into the trees. François and Perrault could not catch him.

"We're an hour late," said Perrault. "We have to leave now. Let's go."

But the team needed Buck. François put Sol-leks back into his old place in the line and called to Buck. Buck watched him from the trees but did not come.

"Put down the club, François," said Perrault.

François put down the club. Then, Buck walked slowly to the head of the line, ready to start work. Now, Buck was the number-one dog.

CHAPTER FOUR

A sad day

Buck and his team worked well together. Every day they traveled many miles over the snow. They came to Skagway quickly, and Perrault was very happy.

Then, Perrault and François had to leave Buck's team and take another team north. François put his arms around Buck and cried. "Goodbye, Buck," he said, sadly. Buck never saw Perrault or François again.

Buck and his team had a new driver on the journey back to Dawson. Many teams of dogs traveled in a line, one after the other. They pulled sleds with heavy bags of letters. The teams left camp early in the morning and traveled all day. At night, the drivers made a new camp, and they gave fish to Buck and the other dogs.

After many days, the dogs were back in Dawson. They were thin and tired, and they really needed to rest for a week. But, after only two days, they had to start back to Skagway. It snowed every day, and it was hard to pull the heavy sleds over new snow. But the drivers looked after their dogs well. Every night, the dogs ate before the men did.

Dave, the old dog in Buck's team, was tired and **weak**, and sometimes he cried with **pain**. His driver talked about him with the other drivers. "Something is wrong inside Dave," he said.

The drivers put their hands in different places on Dave's body, but they could not find anything wrong. But the next day, Dave started falling down. So his driver took him out of his harness and put Sol-leks in Dave's place.

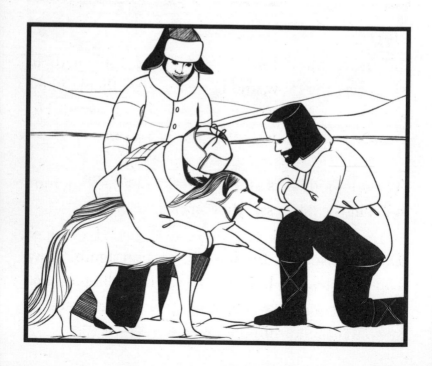

But Dave wanted to work. The dogs pulled their sleds over the snow, and Dave ran after them. They stopped, and Dave found his own team again. He pushed Sol-leks away and stood in his place.

The other drivers stood around Dave. "Put him back in the harness," they said.

Dave's driver put the harness on him again. Now Dave was happy, but then he started falling down. At the camp that evening, the driver made a special place for him by the fire.

The next morning, Dave was very, very weak. He could not get up and lay quietly in the snow. The teams started on their journey, but then they stopped. Dave's driver walked slowly back. He carried a gun in his hands.

The dogs and their drivers waited. Everything was quiet; then there was a loud noise. Buck and all the other dogs knew that noise. Dave was dead. A few minutes later, Dave's driver came back, and the teams started on their journey to Skagway again.

CHAPTER FIVE
A terrible journey

There was no time for rest in Skagway. There were too many letters to take to Dawson. But Buck and his team were too tired and weak for government work. Two men, Charles and Hal, wanted to travel to Dawson, and they needed dogs. They bought Buck and his team and took them to their camp. A pretty young woman waited there. This was Mercedes—Charles's wife and Hal's sister.

Buck watched the two men and the woman, and he did not like them very much. Their camp was very untidy. Charles and Hal started to put all their things on the sled. Some people came and stood around the sled. They wanted to watch.

"The dogs can't pull that sled with all those heavy things," said one man.

"Of course they can," said Hal. "Go!" he shouted. The dogs tried to pull the sled, but it did not move.

"Go, you **lazy** animals!" said Hal. He hit the dogs with a whip. "Go!" he shouted again.

"Those dogs are very tired," said another man. "They need to rest."

"No, they don't," said Hal. "They're lazy." He hit the dogs with the whip again.

"Look," said the man. "There's ice around the sled. You need to break the ice first, and then the dogs can pull the sled."

Hal and Charles broke the ice, and the sled started to move. Boxes and bags fell off the sled and into the snow. Hal fell to the ground, too. Now the sled was lighter, and the dogs ran quickly.

The dogs ran on down the street. Everybody stopped to watch them and to laugh at the two stupid men. Some kind people caught the dogs and brought them back to Hal and Charles.

"You don't need all those things," they said, "and you need more dogs."

Hal and Charles bought six more dogs; now they had fourteen. Buck was the number-one dog in the team, but he was not happy. The new dogs were not strong, and the old dogs were tired. The three people were very lazy, and they could not learn how to work with sleds.

The journey was terrible. Hal wanted the dogs to go faster and travel more miles. He hit them with his whip and his club. But, every day, the team started late because the three people did not get up early. The dogs were hungry because they had to work hard. And, after a time, there was no more food. Charles bought some horse meat, but it was old and bad.

Mercedes grew tired of walking and sat on top of the sled. She was heavy, and it was difficult for the dogs to pull her. But she did not get down.

One of the dogs, Dub, had a bad pain in his leg and could not run very fast. Hal killed him, and some of the other dogs died because they did not have any food to eat. A few days later, Hal killed Billee, too. Now, there were only five dogs.

It was beautiful spring weather. The sun was warm, and the ice in the Yukon River started to break. But Hal and Charles did not understand ice.

At a camp at White River, a man called John Thornton worked. Hal and Charles stopped to talk to him. The dogs fell to the ground and lay there, very tired and weak.

"Don't try to cross the river," said John Thornton. "The ice is breaking, and it's very dangerous."

But Hal and Charles did not want to listen to Thornton.

"We're going to Dawson," said Hal, "and we're going now." He took his whip in his hand. "Get up, Buck!" he said.

But Buck did not move. Hal started hitting him, first with the whip, and then with a heavy club. Buck lay on the ground. He did not feel any pain; there was very little life in him.

"Stop hitting that dog!" said Thornton, angrily. He stood between Hal and Buck. Hal took out his knife, but Thornton hit it with an ax, and the knife fell to the ground. Then, Thornton cut Buck out of his harness.

A few minutes later, the team left the camp and started to cross the river. Buck stayed with Thornton and watched them. There was a loud noise, and the ice broke. Hal, Charles, Mercedes, and the four dogs fell through the ice into the water. They never came up again.

CHAPTER SIX
Happy days

After that day, Buck's life changed. He was very happy with Thornton in his camp by the river. Thornton had two other dogs, and they were friendly. Buck watched the river and listened lazily to the birds. Now he had good food and no work. Slowly, he became strong again, and his fur became thick and beautiful.

Buck had a great love for Thornton, and
Thornton loved Buck, too. Sometimes, Thornton
took Buck's head in his hands and rested his head
on Buck's head. He spoke quietly to Buck, and
Buck listened. He lay at Thornton's feet and
looked up into his face. His love for Thornton
grew stronger every day.

Thornton's friends, Hans and Pete, lived in the
camp, too. One **fall** day, the three friends took a
small boat down the river. Hans and Pete walked
by the river. They held the boat with ropes, and
Buck walked with them. Thornton stood in the
boat and pushed it through the water with a pole.

They came to a difficult place in the river. The water was very fast and strong, and Thornton fell into the river. It carried him quickly toward some rocks. The water around the rocks was **wild** and dangerous, and nobody could swim there. Hans and Pete tied a rope around Buck. Buck jumped into the river and swam toward Thornton. Thornton caught Buck and put his arms around him. Hans and Pete pulled Buck and Thornton slowly through the water. They hit the rocks and went under the water many times before they got out of the river.

Buck lay on the ground. His eyes were closed, and he looked dead. But Thornton spoke quietly to him, and Buck opened his eyes.

———

That winter, in Dawson, Thornton was in a café with some other men. They talked about their dogs.

"My dog is very strong," said one man. "He can pull a sled with five hundred **pounds** on it."

"My dog can pull seven hundred pounds," said another man.

"That's nothing," said Thornton. "My dog Buck can pull a thousand pounds."

All the men in the café looked at Thornton.

"He can't!" said the first man.

"Oh yes, he can!" said Thornton.

The man put some gold on to the table. "Here's a thousand dollars," he said. "My sled is in the street. There are twenty fifty-pound bags of rice on it. That's one thousand pounds. I **bet** you a thousand dollars Buck can't pull that sled."

"All right," said Thornton. But he was worried. Buck was strong, but that was a heavy sled!

Everybody went into the street. Thornton put Buck into his harness and tied him to the sled. There was a lot of hard ice around the sled. Thornton sat down by Buck and took his head in his hands. "Please do this for me, Buck," he said, quietly, in Buck's ear.

Buck started pulling. He pulled and pulled, but the sled was too heavy. He pulled again, and the ice broke and the sled moved. Buck walked slowly down the street with the sled behind him. All the people watched him. "Buck is a really wonderful dog," they said.

Thornton sat down by Buck. He rested his head on Buck's head and started to cry. He spoke quietly to Buck for a long time, and Buck listened happily.

CHAPTER SEVEN
The wolf in the forest

Now, Thornton had a thousand dollars. He and Pete and Hans, with Buck and the other dogs, left Dawson and traveled east through the forest on a long journey. They looked for gold. Summer came, and then another winter.

One day, in the spring, they came to a river, and they could see a lot of gold in the water. This was the end of their journey! They made a camp by the river and started taking the gold from the water. They put it in bags.

There was nothing for Buck or the other dogs to do. Buck lay in the camp in front of the fire. Sometimes he heard a strange **call** from the forest. He did not understand it. It was not the call of a dog.

One night, Buck heard the call again. He jumped up and ran into the forest. He came to an open place in the trees. There he saw a long, gray wolf with its nose pointed to the sky. The call came from the wolf.

Buck went near the wolf, but it was frightened of him and ran away. Buck ran after it. They came to a place in the forest with some high rocks. The wolf stopped and turned. Buck was bigger than the wolf, but he did not want to fight. He touched the wolf's nose with his nose. The wolf became friendly, and started to play. Then, it ran away again, and this time Buck ran with it, side by side.

They ran through the forest, hour after hour. Buck ran by the side of the gray wolf and felt happy. The wolf was like his brother. They stopped by a river to drink. Then, Buck remembered Thornton. The wolf started running again, but Buck did not go with it. He turned and went back to the camp.

Thornton was very happy to see Buck again. The man and the dog played together for a long time. Buck did not leave the camp for two days and nights. He went everywhere with Thornton. He stayed with him at dinner, and at night.

CHAPTER EIGHT

Back to the wild

Some days later, Buck started to hear the call again. Sometimes, he left the camp and slept in the forest at night. He stayed in the forest for days. In the forest, Buck became more and more like a wild animal. He could move very quietly on his stomach. He could catch and kill other animals. Sometimes, he caught fish in the river, too.

One time, Buck stayed in the forest for four days. He went back to the camp, but he **smelled** something bad. Something was very wrong. Everything was very quiet. No birds sang.

Buck found one of Thornton's dogs on the ground. It was dead. Then he found Hans in the long grass. Hans was dead, too.

Buck heard noises. He moved slowly on his stomach toward the camp. There were strange men there, and Buck was very, very angry. He made a terrible noise, attacked the men, and killed some of them. The other men ran into the forest.

Buck found Pete dead in his bed. But Thornton was not in the camp. Buck found his **smell** and went after it to a small river. Thornton was dead in the water. Buck felt a terrible pain and stayed by the river all day. Then night came. The moon was high in the sky, over the trees.

Buck heard the call from the forest. He got up and walked away from the camp and from his life with men. John Thornton was dead. It was time to start a new life—a life in the **wild**.

Some years later, the men in the forest started to tell stories about a strange animal. This animal was like a wolf, but he was not a wolf. He ran with the wolves, but he was bigger and stronger, like a dog. The men were very frightened of this dog-wolf. Sometimes he took their food and killed their dogs. Sometimes he killed men, too.

In the summer, this great dog-wolf visited an old camp by the river. There were no people there, only some old bags of gold. They lay in the grass. The dog-wolf sat by the camp and called a long, sad call.

Then, in the long winter nights, the men saw him again, running at the head of the wolves.

During-reading questions

Write the answers to these questions in your notebook.

CHAPTER ONE

1 Who first took Buck away from his home?
2 What did the four men carry the box on to?
3 What important lesson did Buck learn?

CHAPTER TWO

1 What was Perrault's job?
2 Why did everybody laugh at Buck on the ship?
3 What happened to Curly?

CHAPTER THREE

1 What animal did the dogs see near the camp?
2 Why did Buck attack Spitz?
3 How did Buck become the number-one dog in the team?

CHAPTER FOUR

1 Why was François sad?
2 How many days did the dogs rest in Dawson?
3 How did Dave die?

CHAPTER FIVE

1 Why did Charles and Hal need dogs?
2 How did John Thornton help Buck?
3 What happened to Hal, Charles, and Mercedes?

CHAPTER SIX

1 Who were Hans and Pete?
2 What did Thornton say to some other men that Buck could do?
3 What was on the sled that Buck pulled?

CHAPTER SEVEN

1 What did Thornton and his friends see in the river?
2 Why did Buck go into the forest?
3 What animal did he see there?

CHAPTER EIGHT

1 Who did Buck see in the camp?
2 How did Buck know Thornton was in the river?
3 Why were the men in the forest frightened of the strange dog-wolf?

After-reading questions

1 How did Buck change in the story?
2 What new things did Buck learn?
3 What did Buck think about . . .
   a Spitz
   b Hal, Charles, and Mercedes
   c John Thornton?
4 What do you think about the other dogs in the story?
5 Which people in the story best understood the dogs?
6 Was Buck a good number-one dog in the team? Why/Why not?
7 Does the book have a happy ending or a sad ending, do you think?

Exercises

1 Are these sentences *true* or *false*? Write the correct answers in your notebook.

1 Buck's life with the family was very difficult. ....*false*..........
2 In 1897, people heard about gold in north-west Canada.
3 The men in the Klondike needed big, strong horses.
4 One morning, Manuel took Buck away from his home.
5 Four men carried Buck's box on to a ship.
6 Buck saw a man with a red hat.
7 The man hit Buck with a whip.
8 That day, Buck learned an important lesson.

2 Write the correct answers in your notebook.
Example: 1—b

1 Perrault and François worked for . . .
   a the man in the red shirt
   b the Canadian Government
   c Canadian ships.

2 Which dog tried to take Buck's food?
   a Curly
   b Dave
   c Spitz

3 At first, there were . . . dogs in Perrault's team.
   a three
   b seven
   c nine

CHAPTER THREE

3 **Complete these sentences in your notebook, using the words from the box.**

> thin   attacked   dangerous   jumped   sled
>
> camp   rabbit   team

1 "Good" ice was thick and hard, but "bad" ice was ......*thin*.......

2 "Bad" ice was very .... for the dogs because it broke easily.

3 The dogs pulled the .... across the snow.

4 All the dogs ran after the ....

5 Spitz .... out in front of the rabbit.

6 Buck .... Spitz and broke Spitz's leg.

7 The next morning, Spitz was not in the ....

8 Buck wanted to be the number-one dog in the ....

CHAPTER FOUR

4 **Write the present tense of these verbs in your notebook.**

1 traveled ....*travel*..........	**2** cried	**3** made
4 gave	**5** ate	**6** stopped
7 found	**8** lay	**9** knew

CHAPTER FIVE

5 **Order the story by writing 1–8 in your notebook.**

a ....Hal killed Dub, and some of the other dogs died.

b ....Hal, Charles, Mercedes, and the four dogs fell through the ice.

c ....The team came to John Thornton's camp.

d ....*1*......Charles and Hal bought Buck and his team.

e ....Thornton cut Buck out of his harness.

f ....Charles and Hal put all their things on the sled.

g ....Hal started to hit Buck.

h ....The team started traveling to Dawson.

6 **Who says these words? Write the answers in your notebook.**

Thornton

Hal

1 "Go, you lazy animals!" .... *Hal* ....
2 "Don't try to cross the river."
3 "Get up, Buck!"
4 "Stop hitting that dog!"
5 "Please do this for me, Buck."

7 **Complete these sentences in your notebook, using the question words from the box. Then answer the questions.**

Where	Who	When	How	Which	What	Why

1 ....*Where*.... did Buck live with the family? ....*California*.......
2 .... did people hear about gold in the Klondike? ....
3 .... was "bad ice" dangerous? ....
4 .... dog could not work any more because he was tired and weak? ....
5 .... was Hal's sister? ....
6 .... did Buck get money for Thornton? ....
7 .... did Thornton and his friends find in the river? ....

8 **Match the two parts of the sentences in your notebook.**

Example: 1—c

1	Buck caught and killed animals	**a**	some of the men.
2	Buck stayed in the forest	**b**	the strange dog-wolf.
3	There were strange men	**c**	in the forest.
4	Buck attacked and killed	**d**	for four days.
5	Thornton was dead	**e**	at the head of the wolves.
6	Buck left the camp and started	**f**	in the camp.
7	The men were very frightened of	**g**	in the small river.
8	The dog-wolf ran	**h**	his new life in the wild.

Project work

1 Look online, and find out about a famous dog. Make a poster about your chosen dog.

2 Look online, and find out five interesting things about Canada or Alaska. Think about:

• the people and animals

• the land

• the weather.

Talk to a friend. Say five things about Canada or Alaska that are true, and five things that are not. Ask your friend to guess which things are true. Then listen to your friend, and guess which of the things they say are true.

An answer key for all questions and exercises can be found at
www.penguinreaders.co.uk

Glossary

around (prep.)
on every side of something

attack (v.)
to do something bad to a person.
Often this is because you are
angry with them or you want
something from them.

ax (n.)
You use an *ax* to cut trees.

become (v.)
to start to be something

bet (v.)
to be right and get some money
from a person, or to be wrong
and have to give some money to
a person. People *bet* money on
sports and games.

break (v.)
to *break* something, you hit it
and it goes into small parts

call (n.)
a long, loud noise. You make a
call, and someone hears you.

camp (n.)
You make a *camp* because you
want to eat and sleep and you
are not in a house.

club (n.)
a long, heavy thing. You can
hit things with a *club*.

dangerous (adj.)
A *dangerous* thing can *attack* you.

dead (adj.)
not living

fall (v. and n.)
to go down quickly towards
the ground; the time of year
before winter

fight (v. and n.)
when you hit someone and they
hit you

gold (n.)
People sometimes find hard,
yellow pieces of *gold* in rivers.
Then these people get very
rich. *Gold* is very beautiful, and
people wear it on their bodies.

government (n.)
a group of important people.
They say what must happen in
a country.

harness (n.)
You put a *harness* on an animal.
Then the animal pulls something.

hate (v.)
You *hate* someone because you
do not like them and you are
sometimes angry with them.

ice (n.)
Water starts to be hard because it
is very cold. Then it *becomes ice*.

journey (n.)
when you travel from one place to another place

jump (v.)
to push your body off the ground with your legs and feet

lazy (adj.)
Lazy people and animals do not like working hard.

life (n.)
from the beginning of living, to the end of living. This is a *life*.

line (n.)
When many things are in a *line*, each thing is next to another thing.

mile (n.)
You can run a *mile* in about 7 to 10 minutes. A *mile* is about 1.6 kilometers long.

pain (n.)
when you feel something bad in your body or when you are not well. Sometimes the *pain* is very bad and you cry or shout.

pound (n.)
You use the word *pounds* to say how heavy something is. You can buy a *pound* of apples.

rope (n.)
You use a long, strong *rope* to pull something.

sled (n.)
You use a *sled* to travel across snow. Dogs pull a *sled*.

smell (v. and n.)
You *smell* things with your nose. Dogs can *smell* very well.

team (n.)
a group of people or animals working together

thick (adj.)
Thick ice is strong. If a dog has *thick* fur, it has lots of fur.

thin (adj.)
Thin ice is not strong. It *breaks* when you stand on it.

tie (v.)
to put a *rope* on a thing or animal

weak (adj.)
not strong

whip (n.)
People sometimes use a *whip* to hit slow animals.

wild (n. and adj.)
In the *wild*, there are animals, trees and rivers, but there are no houses. *Wild* water is fast and strong.

Penguin Readers

Visit **www.penguinreaders.co.uk**
for FREE Penguin Readers resources
and digital and audio versions of this book.